HOW TO USE THIS BOOK

1. Put this CD into your CD player.
2. Turn to the first page of the story.
3. Start your CD.
4. When you hear a DING, turn the page.

Pages with this symbol in the upper
right corner mean it's song time! →

If you want to hear the songs by themselves, go to the
second track on your CD and start playing from there.

YOU'RE READY TO JUMP INTO THE POND!

For the little tadpoles in our lives:

Luke

Nicole

Justin

Sari

Fiona

Jasper

&

Christina

PUBLISHED BY ONE WORLD MUSICAL BOOKS

Text Copyright © by Philip Pelletier
Songs Copyright © by Philip Pelletier
Illustrations Copyright © by Verne Lindner

Library of Congress Control Number: 2007922796
ISBN: 978-0-9786176-2-2
Printed in China

One Night in FROGTOWN

In a watery pond
with trees all around,
is a musical place full of frogs
that's called Frogtown.

Now one night in Frogtown
when the peepers were peeping,
Tad played his saxophone
while the tadpoles were sleeping.

Or *trying* to sleep
is what you might say,
because Tad had been playing
all night and all day!

The real reason why
Tad was playing this long?
He heard faraway music
and was playing along.

No one else heard this music
(or believed that you could).
But the truth of it was—
Tad's ears were quite good!

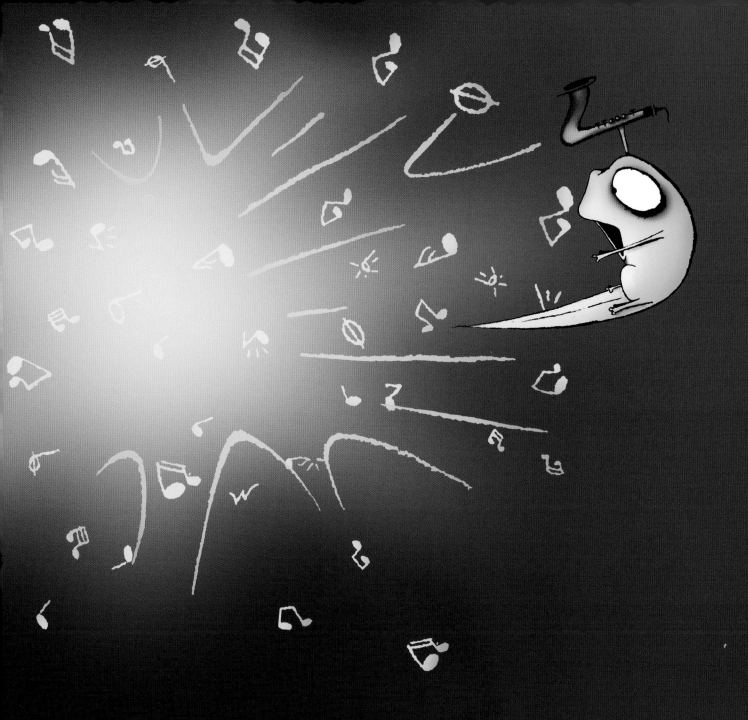

It was way after bedtime;
his friends warned him to stop,
but he went right on playing
'til his bubble went POP!

So off he went swimming,
into the night;
to find the faraway music
under the moonlight.

The first place he found
was a mushroomy cavern—
a blues music club called
The Toadstool Tavern.

MIDDLE OF THE ROAD

We are the Bluesiest
frogs you could meet
and we like to dance
with our webby feet

We've got a toadstool
that grows up from the ground
It's the best mushroom
in all of Frogtown

It's not too high
and it's not too low
it's right in the middle
that's the way to go

No Ifs Ands or Buts!
No Ifs Ands or Buts!
No Ifs Ands or Buts!
and if you ask why?
It's because we said so!

Life is pretty simple
when your toadstool's the best
and blue is the color
that's better than the rest

We've got all the answers
as you can see
you can join our party
as long as you agree

We're not too high
and we're not too low
we're right in the middle
the Middle Of The Road!

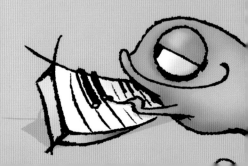

Tad played along and
when they stopped for a rest,
he yelled, "Blues music's fun —
it's one of the best!"

"Blues is the ONLY
real music! You dig?"
said the Bluesfrogs who
suddenly seemed scary and big.

Tad answered, "But..."
They yelled, "No Buts! You see?"
Then they leaned closer,
to make sure he agreed.

Tad sputtered, "But..."
They yelled, "Hear what he said?!"
And the bouncer bounced Tad
out the door- on his head!

Tad thought their actions
were not very kind,
so he kept on swimming to see
who else he could find.

Symphony
Tonite

The next group of frogs
that he happened upon,
all lived in a tree
that grew over the pond.

Classical music's
what they played up in there—
sounds of oboes and trumpets
and flutes filled the air.

ABOVE IT ALL

Although we're quite small
our tree is big and tall
that's how we always stay
Above It All

We live without a care
for those who live down there
relax and breathe the air
Above It All

Oh we know we're the best
who cares about the rest
We are so well dressed
we really must be blessed

Everything is just so
we always make it show
and that is all we know
Above It All

We're the cream of the crop
'cause we're the ones on top
that's why we'll never stop
being Above It All

Afterward Tad said:
"Classical music is fun!"
the Treefrogs all said,
"Classical music's the ONLY one!"

When Tad said he liked
blues music too, they said,
"If you like the blues,
then we don't like you!"

Then they kicked Tad out
of their musical tree,
and that was the end
of his Treefrog Symphony.

"There have got to be frogs
who play music together,
who don't think their music's
the only one ever."

So Tad just kept swimming
on and on 'til he found—
the Lily Pad Club,
in a stump in the ground.

THE DOWN LOW

Up on top
it's too much of a circus
that's why we like it
underneath the surface

All the frogs up there
they simply don't know
that the real party's
always on The Down Low

Our stump is the place to be
It's cool so don't you tell me
It's underground, and VIP
And where it is you can't see

On The Down Low
We keep it in the pocket
On The Down Low
This is where we rock it
On The Down Low
It's full of flies and crickets
On The Down Low
This is where we kick it

I'm a Pondwater Player
you know I'm very tricky
just look at my tongue
it's extremely long and sticky

I can flick it real quick
make it go zoom zoom
I can eat a bug
from across the room

"I love this rap music,"
Tad said with a smile;
"It's one of my favorites
I've heard in a while!"

"Rap music's hip!
Nothing else can compare!
And if you disagree,
then you must be square!"

The Rapfrogs threw Tad
right on out of the stump —
he flew over the lily pads
and fell right on his rump!

Tad let out feelings
he could no longer hide;
somehow that made him
feel better inside.

ALONE

You are all alone
with no place to call home
There's nowhere left to roam
no one to turn to now
No one's going to show you how

You're feeling very small
not so grown up at all
Everywhere you seem to hit a wall
and the rain keeps coming down
doesn't look like it'll stop now

But don't be afraid to sing your song
when it comes from inside
it won't be wrong
Just listen to your heart
feel it getting strong

It's alright to be alone
it's ok to be alone
It's alright to be alone
sometimes you need to be alone

The night can be so cold and blue
the moonlight hidden from view
No one to help you through
all the places you have been
where you don't seem to ever fit in

But inside you there is a place
where tears disappear without a trace
So feel the rain falling on your face
and let your music play
washing all your fears away

One by one slowly
the frogs all joined in —
thinking how stubborn
and close-minded they'd been.

Tad heard them playing
beneath the rainfall,
and realized they weren't
so different after all.

He shouted out,
"Listen to you – it's a start!
You're playing together
instead of apart!"

And just like that
Frogtown changed forever;
all from a tadpole
who said, "Never say never."

FROGTOWN

Frogtown's got all kinds of frogs
some play drums inside of logs
Clarinet players in the trees
rapping underwater MCs
Bullfrogs blowin' on the bass trombone
Tadpoles jammin' on the saxophone

Pollywogs singing in the reeds
webfoot violinists bow in the breeze
Jazz amphibians swing in the lilies
they are serious, don't you see

Frogtown
Where the bugs are juicy
and the water is blue
Frogtown
Where the fish are jumping
and the music is too

Our story here has just been told
like a ripple on the water
making circles of gold
and music beats inside the soul
of even the tiniest tadpole